zen
poems

zen
poems

Manu Bazzano

illustrations: André Sollier

**Andrews McMeel
Publishing**

Kansas City

Design: Balley Design Associates

Editor: Leanne Bryan

ISBN: 0-7407-2379-0

This book is dedicated to my teacher,

Genpo Merzel Roshi.

Acknowledgments

Thank you to the Poetry Library, London, and to the School of Oriental and African Studies, University of London for making their wealth of material available during the research for this book. I am indebted to the whole team at MQ Publications, and in particular to Ljiljana Baird, whose brainchild this anthology really is, and to Leanne Bryan for her infinite patience, kindness and sheer hard work.

contents

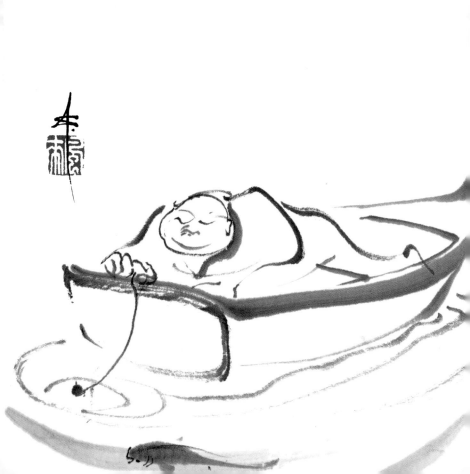

"There is nothing in religion which cannot be found in poetry."

george bataille

Poets are thieves. They steal a fleeting moment of revelation from the ordinary magic that life bestows in great abundance.

Poets deceive us, for in trying to capture in form what is essentially formless, they provide us with an illusion of solidity.

If we then try and combine the elusiveness of poetry with the unfathomable essence of Zen, we are in deep trouble. For what on earth is Zen? Here is a definition given by the 6th century Indian monk Bodhidharma who brought the essential teachings of the Buddha from India to China and who was the first of a long line of Zen Masters:

Outside teaching; apart from tradition,

Not founded on words and letters,

Pointing directly to the human mind,

Seeing into one's nature and attaining Buddhahood.

Faced with the question, Genpo Merzel Roshi, a contemporary American Zen Master, replied: "I don't know." This *not knowing* is as far removed from the ignorance of small-mindedness as it is from the parochial arrogance of those who think that they do know.

On one level, Zen is pure *agnosticism*. An agnostic is one who does not know, one who, without prejudice, is ready to inquire into the nature of reality and one who is willing to explore. Some poetry does exactly that: It ventures out through uncharted territory with courage, humor, and compassion, and in so doing it forces us to reconsider our conditioned view of reality. It invites us to gaze with serenity and equanimity into the abyss, without having to resort to metaphysics, religion, science, or even poetics.

Authentic poetry stumbles into reality by accident. It spells out the threefold manifestations of the divinity, "Truth, Goodness, and Beauty" without having to name the nameless.

I cannot think of a more elusive combination as the one suggested by "Zen poetry." One could settle with the idea that a Zen poem is a poem written by an ancient—or contemporary—practitioner of Zen, expressing in poetic form insights, perceptions, or philosophical and aesthetic musings of a student or of a teacher of the Way. Or we could limit our research to the rich tradition of Japanese haiku poetry.

Attempting to define what today might constitute "Zen poetry" is a temptation against which I will borrow Italian poet Eugenio Montale's dictum: This much I can say, what it is *not*. Zen poetry is not "spiritual." It does not set itself as a poetic version of a spiritual predicament. It does not select "higher" thoughts, it does not prefer "luminous moments" or "epiphanies" to ordinary moments. When the Zen Master Joshu was asked: "What is the Way?" he replied: "Ordinary Mind is the Way," and in expounding and articulating "Dharma Art," the meditation Master Chögyam Trungpa came up with the wonderful formula "First Thought, Best Thought." It is not the overly elaborated, carefully edited verse of the soulless and seasoned wordsmith, but a direct expression of one's heart.

Of course, such an "ordinary mind" might be the most difficult thing to realize, simplicity might be the most arduous undertaking, and "first thought" (a non-dualistic, uncluttered thought—an "original thought" as Nietzsche might have said) the rarest thing in the world.

Zen poetry is not "moral"; it does not try to adorn a series of commandments or precepts. Morality does not serve a sovereign purpose, but purely an utilitarian one: It serves a particular group at a given time in history. Zen poetry *might*—indirectly, accidentally—point at ways to atone.

Authentic poetic sensibility restores the world to its natural fluidity. It questions the very ground on which we stand, undermining our fragile sense of solidity. "Things," as seen through the eyes of the poet, no longer appear as they are. We find something similar in

Zen. At the beginning of her training, the Zen student is said to perceive "mountains as mountains, and rivers as rivers." Form is perceived as form. Halfway through the training, "mountains are no longer mountains, rivers are no longer rivers." Form is perceived as "emptiness." Rather than a series of solid, self-existing, and clearly defined "objects," the world appears to be fluid, without boundaries. We perceive the interconnection of all phenomena. Form is perceived as inherently empty, devoid of intrinsic existence. We are no longer sure of the separation between "self" and "others." For a mature practitioner, "mountains are again mountains, rivers are again rivers," but this time she is also aware of their mutual connection.

Poetry follows a similar trajectory, and in so doing it restores the sacred to the everyday. The world is still there, "mountains are again mountains," but there is a sense of "magic," understood as "full appreciation of chance."

The world is neither glamorized nor rejected by such poetic sensibility. It goes beyond the respectable enslavement of the "court poet," singing to this day from his hired platform the praise of the wealthy and the powerful, or giving "poetic" form to the views in vogue that he will never even dream to challenge. The court poet still lives in the realm of "mountains as mountains, and rivers as rivers." The Zen sensibility also goes beyond the timidity of the "introverted" poet who identifies the external world with greed and evil and retreats into a private mythology, living in the borrowed light of powerful religious archetypes. His is the realm where "mountains are no longer mountains, and rivers no longer rivers." Here the only choice is between drowning in the collective unconscious—which often means madness—or subscribing to a belief system.

Poets such as William Blake walk a wholly different path:

But if at the Church they would give us some Ale,
And a pleasant fire our souls to regale

Dividing poems by seasons is an ancient tradition that runs through Chinese and Japanese poetry. In its more genuine, less formal expressions it testifies of the need to access reality through the only gate available, the gate of the senses. If we do not feel the glory and the fragile, terrifying beauty of the seasons, then we are cut off from reality entirely. We are unable to perceive the basic truth of impermanence:

> A monk asked: "What is the essence of one who is awakened?"
> Joshu said: "Spring, summer, autumn, winter"

A "Zen poem" does not attract attention to itself. It reveals the world as "becoming" without assuming—and this is a crucial point—the existence of "being" behind it. "Impermanence" does not carry a negative judgment. The poet in winter seclusion revels in the beauty of a sudden snowstorm. He does not use the snow and the unpredictability of the weather to pontificate on the evergreen meadows of heaven. He also does not cleverly

enumerate the molecular components of snow, dazzling us with a list of the various tonalities of white. He is neither a spiritualist, nor a "modern" poet. The great haiku poet and Zen practitioner Bashō wrote:

What fun,

it may change into snow—

the winter rain

Such simplicity is the hardest thing to achieve. The season, as R. H. Blyth reminds us, is not seen "as a principle, but as a mode of intuition, a vaster way of seeing particular things." And he adds: "As we look more carefully at the object we see in it the whole world working out its perfect will."

For the content of poetry to assert itself, the poet needs to step aside. In the words of George Barker:

Not in the poet is the poem or

even the poetry. It is hiding behind

a broken wall or a geranium

or walking around pretending to be blind

seeking a home that it cannot find.

Being aware of the changing seasons and listening to the infinitely subtle teachings of "the ten thousand things" is a form of deep appreciation. Poetry then becomes an offering, a prayer, a form of meditation.

manu bazzano

19

spring

spring

All myths of creation originate from this season. Days are longer, and in the daytime, winds sweep the clouds away, heralding change and renewal. Snow and ice melt from the top of the mountains, and rivers come tumbling down in joyful song. The wood pushes through the soil and lovers renew their commitment to passion and tenderness, for spring, as love, is a "deeper season than reason." The fish struggle upstream and everything sparkles like jewels in the new light.

Ice and water,
Their difference resolved,
Are friends again.

yasuhara teishitsu | TR. R. H. BLYTH

In snow thou comest—
Thou shalt go with the resuming ground,
The sweet derision of the crow,
And Glee's advancing sound.

In fear thou comest—
Thou shalt go at such a gait of joy
That man anew embark to live
Upon the depth of thee.

emily dickinson

25

A basket of grass,
And no one there—
Mountains of spring.

masaoka shiki | TR. R. H. BLYTH

Cherry blossoms

Cherry blossoms
Are quiet
Unlike frogs
Leaping to every
Raindrop

zaro weil

26

The myriad differences resolved by sitting, all doors opened.

In this still place I follow my nature, be what it may.

From the one hundred flowers I wander freely,

The soaring cliff — my hall of meditation

(With the moon emerged, my mind is motionless).

Sitting on this frosty seat, no further dream of fame.

The forest, the mountain follow their ancient ways,

And through the long spring day, not even the shadow of a bird.

reizan no tsuki | TR. LUCIEN STRYK

27

First cicada:
life is
cruel, cruel, cruel.

issa kobayashi | TR. LUCIEN STRYK

Will I Listen?

I know a man with something to say.
   Will I listen?

A sudden April wind
    flicks several petals
from a cherrytree I love
    and blows them away.

brendan kennelly

Again far off
that silver tarn
I'll never visit

ken jones

Butterfly
hovers
on my open diary

ken jones

32

This hillside,
the thud of clay on his coffin—
a bird sings.

sean o'connor

The rain is over:
South Mountain puffs out
Spring clouds.

natsume sōseki | TR. SŌIKU SHIGEMATSU

The fish
All struggling upstream:
River in spring.

natsume sōseki | TR. SŌIKU SHIGEMATSU

Song (2)

My gentle hill, I rest
beside you in the dark
in a place warmed by my body,
where by ardor, grace, work,
and loss, I belong.

wendell berry

April Woods: Morning

Birth of color
out of night and the ground.

Luminous the gatherings
of bloodroot

newly risen, green leaf
white flower

in the sun, the dark
grown absent.

wendell berry

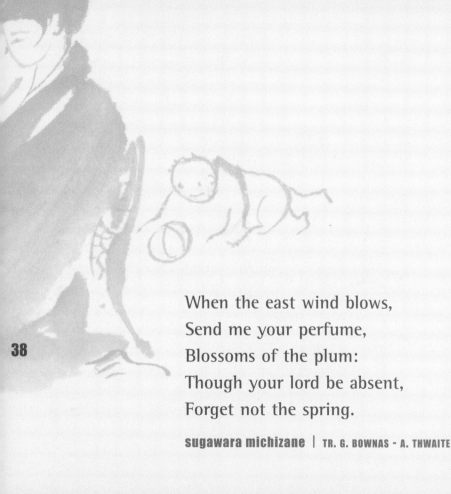

When the east wind blows,
Send me your perfume,
Blossoms of the plum:
Though your lord be absent,
Forget not the spring.

sugawara michizane | TR. G. BOWNAS - A. THWAITE

38

Florence, lily of strength, flower of spring.
Early mornings on the Arno river. The grace of
youth – and no grace is comparable to April's –
alive, innocent, undivided breath. Its coolness
brightens the marbled stone and gives birth to
Botticelli's Venus

dino campana | TR. MANU BAZZANO

Come to the orchard in Spring.
There is light and wine, and sweethearts
in the pomegranate flowers.

If you do not come, these do not matter.
If you do come, these do not matter.

mevlana celaleddin rumi | TR. C. BARKS

After T'ao Ch'ien

"Swiftly the years, beyond recall:
Solemn the stillness of this Spring morning."
I'll put on my boots & old levis
& hike across Tamalpais.
Along the coast the fog hovers,
Hovers an hour, then scatters.
There comes a wind, blowing from the sea,
That brushes the hills of spring grass.

gary snyder

All around is green. Flowers are everywhere.
All particles smile with reflection of Beauty.
Everything sparkles like jewels.
Love and Beloved are united everywhere.

mevlana celaleddin rumi | TR. N. O. ERGIN

43

Spring

bees humming
tires spinning
spring mud

gary snyder

Spring:
A hill without a name
Veiled in morning mist.

matsuo bashō | TR. G. BOWNAS - A. THWAITE

46

The winds of spring
Scattered the flowers
As I dreamt my dream.
Now I awaken,
My heart is disturbed.

priest saigyō | TR. G. BOWNAS - A. TH

yes is a pleasant country:
if's wintry
(my lovely)
let's open the year

both is the very weather
(not either)
my treasure,
when violets appear

love is a deeper season
than reason;
my sweet one
(and april's where we're)

e. e. cummings

Spring Song

As my eyes search the prairie
I feel the summer in the spring.

anonymous, chippewa indian

48

In my begging bowl
Violets and dandelions
Are mixed together:
To the Buddhas of the Three Worlds
I shall offer them.

ryōkan | TR. G. BOWNAS - A. THWAITE

'Kookoorookoo! kookoorookoo!'

'Kookoorookoo! kookoorookoo!'
   Crows the cock before the morn;
'Kikirikee! kikirikee!'
   Roses in the east are born.

'Kookoorookoo! kookoorookoo!'
   Early birds begin their singing;
'Kikirikee! kikirikee!'
The day, the day, the day is springing.

christina rossetti

Spring rain:
Soaking on the roof
A child's rag ball.

yosa buson | TR. G. BOWNAS - A. THWAITE

Weather

52

Morning like an upturned jewel:
A man murmuring with someone at the door—
Birthday of the gods.

nishiwaki junzaburō | TR. G. BOWNAS - A. THWAITE

Fuji alone
Left unburied
By young green leaves.

yosa buson | TR. G. BOWNAS - A. THWAITE

Summer Haiku

Silence

and a deeper silence

when the crickets

hesitate

leonard cohen

Meditate outdoors. The dark trees at night are not really the dark trees at night, it's only the golden eternity.

jack kerouac

Spring Water

Spring water floweth, both to clear and in mud,
my days are but built up calamity; how call this good?

siao min | TR. EZRA POUND

Heaven-Haven

A NUN TAKES THE VEIL

I have desired to go
Where springs not fail,
To fields where flies no sharp and sided hail
And a few lilies blow.

And I have asked to be
Where no storms come,
Where the green swell is in the havens dumb,
And out of the swing of the sea.

gerard manley hopkins

As soon as dawn breaks, young girls go gathering roses. A gust of innocence sweeps through the valleys, the capitals, assist the intelligence of the most vibrant poets, showering down protection for cradles, wreaths for youth, belief in immortality for the aged.

comte de lautreamont | TR. MANU BAZZANO

first spring gust
my flannel shirt
like a kite

shōkan | TR. WILLIAM J. HIGGINSON

coming home
flower
by
flower

60

jane reichhold

Alba

As cool as the pale wet leaves
         of lily-of-the-valley
She lay beside me in the dawn.

ezra pound

Out in the cold sunshine
planting early potatoes
uncertain who I am

ken jones

green grass—
between, between the blades
the color of water

kaga no chiyo | TR. PATRICIA DONEGAN - YOSHIE ISHIBASHI

in and out of our argument a butterfly

brian tasker

64

Bird's Nest

'Tis spring, warm glows the south,
Chaffinch cherries the moss in his mouth
To filbert hedges all day long,
And charms the poet with his beautiful song;
The wind blows bleak o'er the sedgy fen,
But warm the sun shines by the little wood,
Where the old cow at her leisure chews her cud.

john clare

65

World,
Image on water, waves
Break and it is gone, yet
It was

kathleen raine

Butterfly in my hand—
    As if it were a spirit
        Unearthly, insubstantial.

yosa buson | TR. YUZURU MIURA

68

With the cherry blossoms gone
    The temple is glimpsed
        Through twigs and branches.

yosa buson | TR. YUZURU MIURA

A fallen camellia
    On a rock
        In the rapids.

yuzuru miura

Amidst the grassland
Sings a skylark
Free and disengaged from all things

matsuo bashō | TR. YUZURU MIURA

The first morning of spring:
I feel like
someone else

matsuo bashō | TR. R. H. BLYTH

A spring day;
they open the folding doors
of the great temple.

gusai | TR. R. H. BLYTH

74

Sleeping, waking,

And then giving a great yawn,

The cat goes out for lovemaking.

issa kobayashi | TR. YUZURU MIURA

I am one
Who eats his breakfast,
　　Gazing at the morning-glories

matsuo bashō | TR. R. H. BLYTH

Spring MCMXL

London Bridge is falling down, Rome's burnt, and Babylon
The Great is now but dust; and still Spring must
Swing back through Time's continual arc to earth.

david gascoyne

summer

summer

We renew our complicity with life and death, for in summer it's easier to say yes to what is. Happiness is that which happens, and everything moves and breathes in a golden light. In the long twilight of a summer night, we are prone to believe that our wildest dreams can and will become manifest. It is time to go to bed, but. . . that summer moon!

And yet we are also invited to contemplate "summer grasses, all that is left of soldiers' dreams." We wish such splendor and exuberance to be everlasting. Summer imperceptibly makes room for late summer, which the ancient Chinese considered a season in itself: Night downpours haunt our dreams and the dawn appears as if washed anew.

Yonder mountain
Is where the heat of today
Has gone.

uejima onitsura | TR. R. H. BLYTH

A sudden summer shower;
The village sparrows
    Hang on to the grasses.

yosa buson | TR. R. H. BLYTH

Summer sky
Clear after rain—
    Ants on parade.

masaoka shiki | TR. LUCIEN STRYK

mid-day sun
on the gorse
popping seedpods

brian tasker

85

stormy afternoon—
between peals of thunder
the ice-cream van's bell

brian tasker

now in the shower
the maiden's first love
is washed away

shigeru ekuni | TR. WILLIAM J. HIGGINSON

pine shade
the wooden bench
worn smooth

lee gurga

Watering the garden   87
I listen to the soil
whispering in the dark

mirjana božin

Her summer kimono
Loose, untied,
Yet somehow trim.

matsumoto takashi | TR. G. BOWNAS - A. THWAITE

In the summer dusk,
the flickering starlight of
pale topaz glowworms

james kirkup

Last night lightning
this morning
the white iris.

pat donegan

Into the field of
Yellow flowers,
The red setting sun!

natsume sōseki | TR. SŌIKU SHIGEMATSU

Well, it's time
To go to bed, but—
That summer moon.

natsume sōseki | TR. SŌIKU SHIGEMATSU

my way is in the sand flowing

between the shingle and the dune

the summer rain rains on my life

on me my life harrying fleeing

to its beginning to its end

my peace is there in the receding mist

when I may cease from treading these long shifting thresholds

and live the space of a door

that opens and shuts

samuel beckett

To make a prairie it takes a clover and one bee,—
One clover, and a bee,
And revery.
The revery alone will do
If bees are few.

emily dickinson

Summer

When summer came I threw off my shoes
As though to trust
Some promised goodness in the weather.
I grew to love the dust.

I felt each summer slowly yield
To autumn's sensual rust
And thrilled to find my heart at one
With summer dust.

brendan kennelly

Summer night—
I close my eyes
And the cuckoo
With its one cry
Marks the dawn.

ki tsurayuki | TR. G. BOWNAS - A. THWAITE

As if it were a relic
Of the cherry-flowers
Scattered by the storm,
In a waterless sky
A wave billowed.

97

ki tsurayuki | TR. G. BOWNAS - A. THWAITE

Choirboys' Little Chorus (of Joy)

Come on, let's sing.

Sing with joyful breath

The temporary birth

The definitive death.

giorgio caproni | TR. PETER DE VILLE

Accompanying me
through summer fields—
a butterfly

fukada kodojin | TR. J. CHAVES

Summer grasses—
All that remains
Of soldiers' visions.

matsuo bashō | TR. G. BOWNAS - A. THWAITE

100

Night. Moon. Black leaves.
I open the French window wide:
Between us other barriers,
Invisible, infinite.
On my threshold
When my window is open upon the night,
Moths, black leaves, moonlight.

kathleen raine

My Garden – like the Beach –
Denotes there be – a Sea
That's Summer –
Such as These – the Pearls
She fetches – such as Me

emily dickinson

A little Road – not made of Man –
Enabled of the Eye –
Accessible to Thill of Bee –
Or Cart of Butterfly –

If Town it have – beyond itself –
'Tis that – I cannot say –
I only know – no Curricle that rumble there
Bear Me.

emily dickinson

The Sick Rose

O Rose, thou art sick!
The invisible worm
that flies in the night
In the howling storm

Has found out thy bed
of crimson joy
and his dark secret love
Does thy life destroy

william blake

Love me love, til trees fall flat
                their trunks flail down the berries
Til ripe sharp vines crawl through the door
                and the air is full of sparrows

I loved you love, in halls and homes
                and through the long library;
I loved you in the pine and snow
                now I love blackberry

gary snyder

Plum petals falling
cherry still hard buds
drinking wine
in the garden
The landlady comes out
            in the twilight
and beats the rug.

gary snyder

108

Where the bee sucks, there suck I,
In a cowslip's bell I lie,
There I couch when owls do cry,
On the bat's back I do fly
After summer merrily.
Merrily, merrily, shall I live now
Under the blossom that hangs on the bough.

william shakespeare

Firefly lights
 Link up as a chain of beads
  Along the water's edge

kawabata bosha | TR. YUZURU MIURA

A sudden shower—
     I am riding naked
          On a naked horse.

issa kobayashi | TR. YUZURU MIURA

Schematic Nocturne

Fennel, serpent and rush.
Aroma, scent and penumbra.
Air, earth and solitude.

(The ladder reaches to the moon)

federico garcia lorca | TR. STANLEY READ

I love the rest of my life
    Though it is transitory
        Like a light azure morning glory.

tomiyasu fusei | TR. YUZURU MIURA

Bed too short
but long enough
for making love

ken jones

Lifting up their horns,
The cattle look at people
On the summer moor.

seira | TR. R. H. BLYTH

Summer grass;
Along the path to the mountain temple,
Stone images of Buddha.

gojo | TR. R. H. BLYTH

118

A mountain temple;
Clear water running under the verandah,
Moss at the sides.

kitō takai | TR. R. H. BLYTH

The Lily

The modest Rose puts forth a thorn:
The humble Sheep, a threat'ning horn:
While the Lily white shall in Love delight,
Nor a thorn nor a threat stain her beauty bright.

william blake

A fallen flower
flew back to its branch!
No, it was a butterfly

arakida moritake | TR. R. H. BLYTH

The cuckoo—
flies and insects,
listen well!

121

issa kobayashi | TR. S. ADDISS

Someone had to sing,
it was the wind
in the summer park

manu bazzano

So hot
even rocks and trees
shine in my eyes

mukai kyorai | TR. S. ADDISS

End of summer
our pale shadows
escort us to the sea

ken jones

In this world
Even butterflies
Must earn their keep.

issa kobayashi | TR. LUCIEN STRYK

Never forget:
we walk on hell,
gazing at flowers.

issa kobayashi | TR. LUCIEN STRYK

Dragonfly on a rock—
absorbed in
a daydream

santoka taneda | TR. S. ADDISS

Are not the joys of morning sweeter
Than the joys of night,
And are the vig'rous joys of youth
Ashamed of the light?

Let age and sickness silent rob
The vineyards in the night
But those who burn with vig'rous youth
Pluck fruits before the light.

william blake

Town Life

Sun's in the East,
her loveliness
Comes here
To undress.

Twixt door and screen
at moon-rise
I hear
Her departing sighs.

ts'i feng | TR. EZRA POUND

Perfect summer sky—
one blue crayon
missing from the box

evelyn lang

She has put the child to sleep,
And now washes the clothes;
The summer moon.

issa kobayashi | TR. R. H. BLYTH

We wear our sober Dresses when we die,
But Summer, frilled as for a Holiday
Adjourns her sigh—

emily dickinson

Eternity

He who binds to himself a joy
Does the winged life destroy:
But he who kisses the joy as it flies
Lives in eternity's sunrise.

william blake

Ah! Sun-Flower

Ah Sun-flower! weary of time
Who countest the steps of the Sun;
Seeking after that sweet golden clime
Where the traveller's journey is done,

Where the Youth pined away with desire,
And the pale Virgin shrouded in snow;
Arise from their graves and aspire
Where my Sun-flower wishes to go.

william blake

autumn

autumn

No other season reminds us as acutely of impermanence as autumn. No matter how far removed we might be from the natural world, the sight of a fallen leaf reminds us that nothing lasts for long. Everything that is born is subject to decay. And still, the fall is alight with a mysterious glow. The exuberance of summer is over, for "beauty's charm is but a few days' dream." Autumn invites reflection and forbearance but can also tickle our somber mood by presenting us with a dazzling display of sunshine and warmth.

After R. M. Rilke

Lord, it's time; the wine is already fermenting.
The time has come to have a home,
Or to remain for a long time without one.
The time has come not to be alone,
Or else we will stay alone for a long time.
We will consume the hours over books,
Or in writing letters to distant places,
Long letters from our solitude.
And we will go back and forth through the street
Restless, while the leaves fall.

primo levi

Morning glory:
A beauty's charm
But a few day's dream.

natsume sōseki | TR. SŌIKU SHIGEMATSU

The one great pearl is always present.
Dragon sons and daughters
Are always born of dragon parents.
But how can it be spoken of?
The rains have passed,
And the autumn river runs deep and fast.

zen koan

Of Yellow was the outer Sky
In Yellower Yellow hewn
Till Saffron in Vermillion slid
Whose seam could not be shewn.

emily dickinson

144 Opening their mouths,
They await the parent birds
In the autumn rain.

issa kobayashi | TR. R. H. BLYTH

Gathered together
with the swept-up chestnuts—
fallen leaves

fukada kodojin | TR. J. CHAVES

Garden gate
suddenly banging shut—
autumn wind

fukada kodojin | TR. J. CHAVES

Returning At Night

Soughing, soughing, leaves in the empty wood;
from the deserted village, one lamplight, dim.
The traveler sees not a single shadow;
Somewhere a dog barks at the cold stars

fukada kodojin | TR. J. CHAVES

Half Moon

The moon goes over the water.
How tranquil the sky is!
She goes scything slowly
the old shimmer from the river;
meanwhile a young frog
takes her for a little mirror.

federico garcia lorca | TR. W. B. MERWIN

In an old pond a frog ages while leaves fall

yosa buson | TR. THOMAS RIMER

I waited and I
Yearned for you.
My blind
Stirred at the touch
Of the autumn breeze.

princess nukada | TR. G. BOWNAS - A. THWAITE

150

In the dew dripping
On the broad-flanked hill,
Waiting for you
I stood dampened
By the dew of the hill.

prince ōtsu | TR. G. BOWNAS - A. THWAITE

Night

Candle, lamp,
lantern and firefly.

The constellation
of the dart.

Little windows of gold
trembling,
and cross upon cross
rocking in the dawn.

Candle, lamp,
lantern and firefly.

federico garcia lorca | TR. JAIME DE ANGULO

Autumn sees the plants wither,
wild beauties decline together;
all things cold now as pain,
I turn to go home again.

siao min | TR. EZRA POUND

The grasses and trees
Change their colours;
But to the wave-blooms
On the broad sea-plain
There comes no autumn.

bunya yasuhide | TR. G. BOWNAS - A. THWAITE

154

A man without feelings,
Even, would know sadness
When snipe start from the marshes
On an autumn evening.

priest saigyō | TR. G. BOWNAS - A. THWAITE

155

On Evergreen Hill
Where no tree turns crimson,
The deer that haunt there
By their own belling
May know autumn has come.

ōnakatomi yoshinobu | TR. G. BOWNAS - A. THWAITE

No man lives now
In the warden's house
By the Fuwa Barrier,
Its timbers rotten:
Only autumn's winds.

fujiwara yoshitsune | TR. G. BOWNAS - A. THWAITE

159

lamplit room
the spider
stretches its shadow

brian tasker

On a bare branch
A rook roosts:
Autumn dusk.

matsuo bashō | TR. G. BOWNAS - A. THWAITE

Wind and Silver

Greatly shining,
The Autumn moon floats in the thin sky;
And the fish-ponds shake their backs and
    flash their dragon scales
As she passes over them.

amy lowell

163

persimmons
lightly swaying—
heavy with
themselves

virginia brady young

164

the red ribbon award
for my first sunflower
has faded to orange

kam holifield

early morning wind in the umbrella of the pumpkin stand

marlene mountain

picking the last pears
yellow windows hang
in the dusk

ruth yarrow

Autumn in gaol

In autumn a friend
Sent in an apple.
I made to eat it
All at once.
Red: too red.

In my palm, heavy:
Heavy as the world.

tsuboi shigeji | TR. G. BOWNAS - A. THWAITE

By fading torchlight
squeezing out
the last of my toothpaste

ken jones

At an old temple
In the depths of Takano
In the province of Ki,
I spend the night listening
To raindrops through the cedars.

ryōkan | TR. DONALD KEENE

Thunder moth

After the thunder
The thunder moth comes to the village.
Covered with the pollen of the lilies
In the village headman's garden,
She flutters a little
By the police box at the crossroads.
Then, lofted on the wind,
She soars higher than the pasanias,
Higher than the alarm bell
Of the fire-tower.

miyoshi tatsuji | TR. G. BOWNAS - A. THWAITE

moonlight gleaming
on the grapes—the lovers
can't stop laughing

penny harter

It rains in my heart
As it rains on the town:
What is this languorous ache
That wounds my heart?

Gentle, the sound of rain
Battering roof and ground.
How sweet the sound of rain
For the heart in pain!

paul verlaine | TR. MANU BAZZANO

My Heart at Evening

At nightfall you hear the bat shriek.

Two black horses leap across the meadow.

A red maple rustles.

Along the way a small tavern appears to the traveler.

The young wine and nuts are delicious.

It is wonderful to stagger, drunk, through the darkening forest.

Through black branches comes the ringing of grieving bells.

Dew covers your face.

georg trakl | TR. MANU BAZZANO

This little house
No smaller than the world
Nor I lonely
Dwelling in all that is.

kathleen raine

175

A thousand clouds among a myriad streams
And in their midst a person at his ease.
By day he wanders through the dark green hills,
At night goes home to sleep beneath the cliffs.
Swiftly the changing seasons pass him by,
Tranquil, undefiled, no earthly ties.
Such pleasures!—and on what do they rely?
On a quiet calm, like autumn river water.

hanshan | TR. PETER HARRIS

My beloved friend
You and I had a sweet talk,
Long ago, one autumn night.
    Renewing itself,
The year has rumbled along,
That night still in memory.

ryōkan | TR. NOBUYUKI YUASA

No one believes that death is the end,
If after a day's harvesting he sees the sheaves shine
And the grain smile as it pours into his hand

rené char | TR. MANU BAZZANO

Evening coming—
   the office girl
Unloosing her scarf.

jack kerouac

No, it is not in that lake among crags,
Nor on that expansive and foaming sea-shore,
Nor in the ideal forest full of fears
That I watch myself and go to ponder.

It is here, in this room of a house,
Here among walls without landscape,
That I see romanticism – wing
Of what I didn't know of myself – take its flight.

It is in us that there are all the lakes and forests
If we see clearly into what we are,
It's not because the waves may break
The green blank edges […]

fernando pessoa | JAMES GREENE - CLARA DE AZEVEDO MAFRA

181

The vine among the rocks
Heavy with grapes
the shadows of September
among the gold glint of the grass
among shining
willow leaves the small birds moving
silent in the presence of a new season

denise levertov

182

in the sound
of cutting firewood
the autumn heavens go dark

shinkū fukuda | TR. WILLIAM J. HIGGINSON

Through a hole
in a borrowed tent
the Milky Way

steve shapiro

autumn drizzle—
the slow ticking
of the clock

bruce ross

Cloud maps shift across
a windy sky, as unknown
countries ebb and flow.

francis howell

From within the nostrils
    Of the colossal Buddha
        Comes out this morning's fog.

issa kobayashi | TR. YUZURU MIURA

186

Fall, leaves, fall; die, flowers, away;
Lengthen night and shorten day;
Every leaf speaks bliss to me
Fluttering from the autumn tree.

I shall smile when wreaths of snow
Blossom where the rose should grow;
I shall sing when night's decay
Ushers in a drearier day.

emily brontë

A rust and polished
Pheasant
Swoops low
Through mist
With shrills
To clear his path

zaro weil

Oh, cricket!
Act as the grave keeper
After I'm gone.

issa kobayashi | TR. YUZURU MIURA

twilight
staples rust
in the telephone pole

alan pizzarelli

190

A woodpecker's drilling
Echoes
To the mountain clouds

iida dakotsu | TR. YUZURU MIURA

How beautiful—
Red peppers
After the autumn gale.

yosa buson | TR. YUZURU MIURA

Insects are crying;
The moon comes out,
The garden is yet darker.

masaoka shiki | TR. R. H. BLYTH

Traceless, no more need to hide.
Now the old mirror
Reflects everything—autumn light
Moistened by faint mist.

suian | TR. LUCIEN STRYK

Kittens
playing hide and go seek
in the bushclover

issa kobayashi | TR. S. ADDISS

Hallowe'en

It is Hallowe'en. Turnip Head
Will soon be given his face,
A slit, two triangles, a hole.
His brains litter the table top,
A candle stub will be his soul.

michael longley

197

winter

winter

The winter seclusion as experienced by poets in China or Japan is largely unknown to us: silence and a deeper silence, shrouded in layers of snow. In the modern world winter is "the season of comfort." And yet we feel our energies waning with the light. "It gets dark at four o'clock" and "the windshield is filled with night and cold." Nights are long, and nature's stillness invites us to venture into the darkness without a light, for that is the only way to know darkness: "I won't even take the lantern," for "the dark is so dark, there's no obscurity."

Winter reminds us of old age and death, but we still find a way to be playful: "What fun, it may change into snow—the winter rain." In the heart of such deep stillness we find the quivering seeds of the new season, and in our own hearts the strength to trust in the constant flow of life, for "at the height of the storm there is always a bird to reassure us. An unknown bird," who "sings before flying away."

A shimmering ice bird
    floats down river
Winter's unexpected gift

john daido loori

Frozen snow
　　adorns the naked tree
flowers bloom in winter.

john daido loori

203

Cold moon—
echoing in the withered trees
a waterfall

fukada kodojin | TR. J. CHAVES

the far shore
drifting out of the mist
to meet us

elizabeth searle lamb

206

windblown Christmas lights—
still place
between stars

ruth yarrow

two soap bubbles
across the square
in the late winter sun

subhaga failla

Bearing the Light

Rain-diamonds, this winter morning,
embellish the tangle of unpruned
pear-tree twigs; each solitaire,
placed, it appears, with considered
judgement, bears the light
beneath the rifted clouds—the indivisible
shared out in endless abundance.

denise levertov

February 2, 1968

In the dark of the moon, in flying snow, in the dead of winter,
war spreading, families dying, the world in danger,
I walk the rocky hillside, sowing clover.

wendell berry

Seeing The Unseen

Snow, large flakes,
whirling in midnight air,
unseen, coming to rest
on a fast-asleep, very small village
set among rocky fields; not one
lit square of wakeful window

denise levertov

I fear winter because it is the season of comfort.

arthur rimbaud | TR. MANU BAZZANO

Fog

The fog comes
on little feet.

It sits looking
over harbor and city
on silent haunches
and then moves on.

carl sandburg

The hare jumps
Across the
White frost field
So smooth
So sure
A summer river

zaro weil

What is your
Original Nature,
Snowman?

natsume sōseki | TR. SŌIKU SHIGEMATSU

The Lantern

I won't even take
the lantern. There
the dark's so dark
there's no obscurity

giorgio caproni | TR. MANU BAZZANO

What does this day bestow?
Beauty of sparse snow
Whose wet flakes touch
The soil, then vanish

kathleen raine

Winter under cultivation
Is as arable as Spring.

emily dickinson

Then and Now

In younger days I was happy in the morning,
wept in the evening; now that I am older, I begin
my day in doubt, but its end is holy to me and
serene.

friedrich holderlin | TR. MICHAEL HAMBURGER

Like a day of rest is the end of the year,
Like a question's tone that seeks completion.

friedrich holderlin | TR. MICHAEL HAMBURGER

Crowcolour

Crow was so much blacker
Than the moon's shadow
He had stars.

He was as much blacker
Than any negro
As a negro's eye-pupil.

Even, like the sun,
Blacker
Than any blindness.

ted hughes

Dark At Four O'Clock

It gets dark at four o'clock now

The windshield is filled with night and cold

the motor running for the heater's sake

We finally forgive ourselves

and touch each other between the legs

At last I can feel the element of welcome in our kisses

leonard cohen

shorter kisses
longer quarrels—
winter solstice

eric amann

Life on its way returns into a mist,
Its quickness is its quietness again:
Existence of this world of things and men
Renews their never needing to exist.

lao tzu

222

Moonlit sleet

In the holes of my

Harmonica

david lloyd

Rain beating down
On top of snow.
Add any more and my heart
Melts, melts, melts.

muromachi ballad | TR. G. BOWNAS - A. THWAITE

Thick window frost—

through a melted finger hole

blue sky

223

david elliot

New Year's Day
Dawns clear, and sparrows
Tell their tales.

hattori ransetsu | TR. G. BOWNAS - A. THWAITE

226

What fun,
it may change into snow—
the winter rain

matsuo bashō | TR. R. H. BLYTH

The wind has the rain
in its teeth; gallops off like
a dog with a bone.

francis howell

Winter burial:
a stone angel points his hand
at the empty sky

eric amann

In a single night
The storm-wind came
And built high up
This mound of sand.
Whose grave is it?

ishikawa takuboku | TR. G. BOWNAS - A. THWAITE

Snow
falls on snow—
silence

santoka taneda | TR. S. ADDISS

The wind in the pines
Soughs night and day
In the ears of the stone horse
At a mountain shrine
Where no man worships.

ishiwaka takuboku | TR G. BOWNAS - A. THWAITE

winter sunset—
long shadows follow us home
from the sledding hill

patricia neubauer

In the winter lamp,
Dead face not far
From the living face.

iida dakotsu | TR. G. BOWNAS - A. THWAITE

Now the warriors of winter they gave a cold triumphant shout
And all that stays is dying and all that lives is camping out
See the geese in chevron flight flapping and racing on
  before the snow

joni mitchell

234

In my medicine cabinet
  the winter fly
has died of old age.

jack kerouac

Dragonfly

Dragonfly
Dead on the snow
How did you come so high
Did you leave your seed child
In a mountain pool
Before you died

gary snyder

235

New Year's Eve—
my mind wanders over
ancestors' graveyard.

kretić milivoje | TR. WILLIAM J. HIGGINSON

236

Here and there in the cemetery
dew
like the bones of January.

ana rosa núñez | TR. WILLIAM J. HIGGINSON

To Know The Dark

To go in the dark with a light is to know the light.
To know the dark, go dark. Go without sight,
and find that the dark, too, blooms and sings,
and is traveled by dark feet and dark wings.

wendell berry

238

At the height of the storm, there is always a   **239**
bird to reassure us.
An unknown bird. He sings before flying away.

rené char | TR. MANU BAZZANO

winter evening
the sheep stand still together
in the darkening

marcel smets | TR. WILLIAM J. HIGGINSON

240

A child shakes
the first snow from the swing.
A quiet morning.

tomislav maretić | TR. WILLIAM J. HIGGINSON

a cold room
the shape of the last guest
in the empty chair

martin lucas

Reply to a Friend's Letter

Your smoky village is not so far from here
But icy rain kept me captive all morning.
Just yesterday, it seems, we passed an evening together
     discussing poetry
But it's really been twenty windblown days.
I've begun to copy the text you lent me,
Fretting how weak I've become.
This letter seals my promise to take my staff
And make my way through the steep cliffs
As soon as the sun melts the ice along the mossy path.

ryōkan | TR. JOHN STEVENS

Solitude

There is a charm in solitude that cheers,
A feeling that the world knows nothing of;
A green delight the wounded mind endears
After the hustling world is broken off,
Whose whole delight was crime – at good to scoff.
Green solitude, his prison, pleasure yelds,
The bitch fox heeds him not; birds seem to laugh.
He lives the Crusoe of his lonely field
Whose dark green oaks his noontide leisure shield.

john clare

Sitting on my hat,
on a damp bench, my idle
thoughts range far and wide.

francis howell

Night Crow

When I saw that clumsy crow
Flap from a wasted tree,
A shape in the mind rose up:
Over the gulfs of dream
Flew a tremendous bird
Further and further away
Into a moonless black,
Deep in the brain, far back.

theodore roethke

The sleet falls
  As if coming through the bottom
    Of loneliness.

naitō jōsō | TR. YUZURU MIURA

248

In the darkest hour
before the dawn, feathered voices
talk of sudden death.

francis howell

Resigned to death by exposure,
 How the wind
  Cuts through me!

matsuo bashō | TR. YUZURU MIURA

 Heaven and earth   249
  Convulsing in the same breath
   Let fall a tremendous snow.

 nozawa setsuko | TR. YUZURU MIURA

Acknowledgments

George Barker: "Not in the poet" 5 lines from his *Villa Stellar*, (Faber and Faber, 1978) by permission of the publisher. Matsuo Bashō: "What fun" translated by Stephen Addiss from *A Haiku Garden*, (Weatherhill, 1996) by permission of the translator; "Amidst the grassland," "Resigned to death" translated by Yuzuru Miura from *Classic Haiku* (Charles E. Tuttle Co., Inc. of Boston, Massachusetts and Tokyo, Japan, 1991) by permission of the publisher; "Spring," "Summer grasses," "On a bare branch" from *The Penguin Book of Japanese Verse* (Penguin Books, 1964) Translation copyright © 1964 by Geoffrey Bownas and Anthony Thwaite. By permission of the publisher. Samuel Beckett: "My way is in the sand flowing" from his *Poems In English* (John Calder Publishers Ltd., 1961) by permission of the publisher. Wendell Berry: "April Woods: Morning," "February 2, 1968," "Song (2)," "To Know the Dark" from *Collected Poems: 1957-1982* by Wendell Berry. Copyright © 1985 by Wendell Berry. Reprinted by permission of North Point Press, a division of Farrar, Straus and Giroux, LLC. Kawabata Bosha: "Firefly lights" translated by Yuzuru Miura from *Classic Haiku* (Charles E. Tuttle Co., Inc. of Boston, Massachusetts and Tokyo, Japan, 1991) by permission of the publisher. Mirjana Božin: "Watering the garden" by permission of the author. Yosa Buson: "In an old pond" translated by Thomas Rimer from *The Classic Tradition of Haiku* ed. Faubion Bowers (Dover Publications Inc., 1996) by permission of the translator; "With the cherry blossoms gone," "Butterfly," "How beautiful" translated by Yuzuru Miura from *Classic Haiku* (Charles E. Tuttle Co., Inc. of Boston, Massachusetts and Tokyo, Japan, 1991) by permission of the publisher; "Spring Rain," "Fuji alone" from *The Penguin Book of Japanese Verse* (Penguin Books, 1964) Translation copyright © 1964 by Geoffrey Bownas and Anthony Thwaite. By permission of the publisher. Giorgio Caproni: "Choirboys' Little Chorus (of Joy)" translated by Peter De Ville from Kings College London's *Modern Poetry In Translation* No. 15, New Series, copyright © Modern Poetry In Translation 1999, by permission of the publisher. Leonard Cohen: "Dark at Four O'clock" from his *Stranger Music*, (Jonathan Cape, 1993) copyright © 1993 by Leonard Cohen; "Summer Haiku" from his *Selected Poems*, (Jonathan Cape, 1969) copyright © 1964, 1966, 1968 by Leonard Cohen, by permission of the author. E. E. Cummings: "yes is a pleasant country" is reprinted from *Complete Poems 1904-1962*, by E. E. Cummings, edited by George J. Firmage, by permission of W. W. Norton & Company, Copyright © by the Trustees for the E. E. Cummings Trust and George James Firmage. Ilda Dakotsu: "In the winter lamp" from *The Penguin Book of Japanese Verse* (Penguin Books, 1964) Translation copyright © 1964 by Geoffrey Bownas and Anthony Thwaite. By permission of the publisher; "A woodpecker's drilling" translated by Yuzuru Miura from *Classic Haiku* (Charles E. Tuttle Co., Inc. of Boston, Massachusetts and Tokyo, Japan, 1991) by permission of the publisher. Patricia Donegan: "Last night lightening" reprinted her *Without Warning* (1990) by Pat Donegan by permission of the author and Parallax Press, Berkeley, California, www.Parallax.org. David Elliot: "Thick window frost" from his *Wind In The Trees* (AHA Books, 1992) Copyright © 1992 by David Elliot, by permission of the author. Subhaga Failla: "two soap bubbles" by permission of the author. Shinkū Masahisa Fukada: "in the sound" translated by William J. Higginson from his *Haiku World* (Kodansha International, copyright © 1996) by permission of the author and the translator. David Gascoyne: "Spring MCMXL" 3 lines from his *Collected Poems*, Copyright © 1965, 1988 by David Gascoyne (Oxford University Press, 1988) by permission of Judy Gascoyne. Lee Gurga: "pine shade" from his *In and Out of Fog* (Press Here, © 1997 by Lee Gurga) by permission of the author. Penny Harter: "moonlight gleaming" from her *Stages and Views* (Katydid Books, copyright © 1974), reprinted in William J. Higginson *Haiku World* (Kodansha International, 1996) by permission of the author. Friedrich Holderlin: "Then and Now" and an excerpt from "Winter" are taken from *Holderlin: Selected Verse* translated by Michael Hamburger (Anvil

Press Poetry, 1986) by permission of the publisher. Kam Holifield: "the red ribbon award" from her *After Lights Out* (Spring Street Haiku Group Chapbooks, 1996) by permission of the author. Francis Howell: "Sitting on my hat," "Cloud maps," "In the darkest hour," "The wind" by permission of the author. Ted Hughes: "Crowcolour" from his *Crow*, Copyright © 1970, 1972 by Ted Hughes (Faber and Faber, 1972) by permission of the publisher. Ken Jones: "Butterfly," "Bed too short," "Again far off," "End of summer," "Out in the cold sunshine," "By fading torchlight" from *Pilgrim Foxes* (Pilgrim Press, Troed Rhiw Sebon, Cwmrheidol, Aberystwyth, SY23 3NB, Wales, UK 2001) by permission of the author. Naitō Jōsō: "The sleet" translated by Yuzuru Miura from *Classic Haiku* (Charles E. Tuttle Co., Inc. of Boston, Massachusetts and Tokyo, Japan, 1991) by permission of the publisher. Nishiwaki Junzaburō: "Weather" from *The Penguin Book of Japanese Verse* (Penguin Books, 1964) Translation copyright © 1964 by Geoffrey Bownas and Anthony Thwaite. By permission of the publisher. Kaga no Chiyo: "green grass" translated by Patricia Donegan and Yoshie Ishibashi from *Chiyo-ni: Woman Haiku Master* (Charles E. Tuttle Co., Inc. of Boston, Massachusetts and Tokyo, Japan, 1996) by permission of the publisher. Brendan Kennelly: "Summer" from his *Breathing Spaces*, (Bloodaxe Books, 1992) copyright © 1966, 1967, 1968, 1972, 1973, 1974, 1977, 1979, 1980, 1982, 1992 by Brendan Kennelly; "Will I listen?" from his *Poetry My Arse*, (Bloodaxe Books,1995) copyright © 1995 by Brendan Kennelly, by permission of the publisher. Issa Kobayashi: "The cuckoo," "Kittens" translated by Stephen Addiss from *A Haiku Garden*, (Weatherhill, 1996) by permission of the translator. "First cicada," "Never forget," "In this world" translated by Lucien Stryk from *Where We Are* (Skoob Books Ltd., 1997) by permission of the translator; "Sleeping, waking," "A sudden shower," "From within the nostrils," "Oh, cricket!" translated by Yuzuru Miura from *Classic Haiku* (Charles E. Tuttle Co., Inc. of Boston, Massachusetts and Tokyo, Japan, 1991) by permission of the publisher. Fukada Kodojin: "Accompanying me," "Gathered together," "Garden gate," "Cold moon" translated by Stephen Addiss from *Old Taoist: the life, art, and poetry of Kodojin* (Columbia University Press, 2000) by permission of the translator; "Returning" translated by Jonathan Chaves from *Old Taoist: the life, art, and poetry of Kodojin* (Columbia University Press, 2000) by permission of the translator. Mukai Kyorai: "So hot" translated by Stephen Addiss from *A Haiku Garden*, (Weatherhill, 1996) by permission of the translator. Evelyn Lang: "perfect summer sky" copyright © 1993 by Evelyn Lang from *Modern Haiku* vol. XXIV/3, by permission of the author. Denise Levertov: "Bearing the Light", "Seeing the Unseen" from her *Sands of the Well*, copyright © Estate of Denise Levertov 1994, 1995, 1996, 1998 (Bloodaxe Books, 1998) by permission of the publisher. Primo Levi: "After R. M. Rilke" translated by Ruth Feldman and Brian Swann from *Collected Poems* by Primo Levi (Faber and Faber, 1988) by permission of the publisher. David Lloyd: "Moonlit sleet" first published in *Haiku Magazine* vol. 4, 1970, copyright © 1970 by Eric Amann, by permission of the author. Michael Longley: "Hallowe'en" from his *Selected Poems* (Jonathan Cape, 1998) copyright © by Michael Longley 1998, by permission of the author. John Daido Loori: "A shimmering," "Frozen snow" from his *Making Love with Light* (Dharma Communications, 2000) by permission of the publisher. Federico Garcia Lorca: "Night" translated by Jaime De Angulo, "Schematic Nocturne" translated by Stanley Read, "Half Moon" translated by W. S. Merwin from *The Selected Poems of Federico Garcia Lorca* (copyright © 1955 by New Directions Publishing Corp.) reprinted by permission of New Directions Publishing Corp. Martin Lucas: "a cold room" from *Haiku World* ed. William J. Higginson (Kodansha International, 1996) by permission of the author. Tomislav Maretić: "A child shakes" translated by William J. Higginson from his *Haiku World* (Kodansha International, copyright © 1996) by permission of the author and the translator. Sugawara Michizane: "When the east wind blows" from *The Penguin Book of Japanese Verse* (Penguin Books, 1964) Translation copyright © 1964 by Geoffrey Bownas and Anthony Thwaite. By permission of the publisher. Kretić Milivoje: "New Year's Eve" translated by William J. Higginson from his *Haiku World* (Kodansha International, copyright © 1996) by permission of the translator. Siao Min: "Spring water

252

Author index

255